GROW THROUGH IT

GROW THROUGH IT

INSPIRATION FOR WEATHERING LIFE'S SEASONS

DANI DIPIRRO

LOM
ART

First published in Great Britain in 2020 by LOM ART, an imprint of
Michael O'Mara Books Limited
9 Lion Yard
Tremadoc Road
London SW4 7NQ

Published by arrangement with TarcherPerigee, an imprint of Penguin Publishing Group,
a division of Penguin Random House LLC

A CIP catalogue record for this book is available from the British Library.

Papers used by Michael O'Mara Books Limited are natural, recyclable products made from wood
grown in sustainable forests. The manufacturing processes conform to the environmental
regulations of the country of origin.

ISBN: 978-1-912785-39-1 in hardback print format

1 2 3 4 5 6 7 8 9 10

Printed in Germany

www.mombooks.com

GROW THROUGH IT

NO MATTER
WHAT THE SEASON,
KEEP GROWING...

SEASONS HAVE ALWAYS PLAYED A STARRING ROLE IN MY LIFE. THEY SHAPE WHAT'S CURRENTLY HAPPENING AROUND ME AND CREATE A PATH FOR WHAT NEEDS TO BE DONE IN THE MONTHS TO COME. THEY HAVE UNINTENTIONALLY PROVIDED MY LIFE WITH A STEADY RHYTHM AND, OVER TIME, I'VE LEARNED A GREAT DEAL FROM PAYING ATTENTION TO HOW THE SEASONS ARE A REFLECTION OF MY OWN PROGRESS AND GROWTH. THIS BOOK IS FILLED WITH THE INSIGHTS I'VE GAINED SO FAR, DESIGNED TO HELP YOU FLOURISH AND THRIVE IN EVERY SEASON OF LIFE.

SEASONAL METAPHORS FREQUENTLY REFER TO THE VARIOUS TIMES OF YEAR AS PHASES OF OUR LIVES (YOUTH AS SPRING, OLD AGE AS WINTER), BUT IN THIS BOOK WE'RE GOING TO EXPLORE THE SEASONS NOT AS LIFE STAGES BUT AS EMOTIONAL STAGES. WE'LL EXPLORE THE EMOTIONAL EXPERIENCES OF EACH SEASON (THE UPS AND THE DOWNS!), AND I'LL SHARE INSPIRATION ON HOW TO GROW THROUGH EACH ONE.

THE TRICK TO UNDERSTANDING AND GROWING THROUGH YOUR EMOTIONAL SEASONS COMES FROM KNOWING WHAT TO LOOK FOR – AND HOW TO APPLY THAT WISDOM TO YOUR LIFE. I'VE FOUND IT HELPFUL TO FOCUS ON THE THREE MAIN INSIGHTS SEASONS CAN OFFER US: ACCEPTANCE, BALANCE, AND CHANGE.

ACCEPTANCE

TAKING NOTE OF STRENGTHS AND WEAKNESSES TEACHES US TO ACCEPT, RATHER THAN RESIST, WHAT IS. CHANGING SEASONS REMIND US THAT EVERYTHING IS FLEETING. ACCEPTING THIS ISN'T ALWAYS EASY, BUT LEARNING TO DO SO WILL HELP YOU WEATHER EVERY ASPECT OF YOUR LIFE.

BALANCE

EACH SEASON YOU EXPERIENCE HAS ITS HIGHS AND LOWS, BUT BOTH ARE NECESSARY FOR GROWTH. EVERYTHING THAT HAPPENS (GOOD OR BAD) INFLUENCES WHAT HAPPENS NEXT. THE MORE YOU NOTICE HOW EVERYTHING IS CONNECTED, THE MORE WISDOM YOU'LL GATHER FROM EVERY EXPERIENCE YOU ENCOUNTER.

CHANGE

SEASONS ARE A PHYSICAL REMINDER OF CHANGE. CHANGE CAN BE UNPLEASANT, BUT AS YOU GO THROUGH LIFE'S SEASONS AND STRIVE TO UNDERSTAND YOURSELF WITHIN THEM, CHANGE BECOMES EASIER. RATHER THAN WISH FOR IT TO BE SUMMER, YOU'LL LEARN TO LOOK FOR THE INSPIRATION IN YOUR WINTERS.

YOU'LL LEARN MORE ABOUT EACH SEASON IN ITS INDIVIDUAL SECTION, BUT HERE'S WHEN YOU MIGHT WANT TO TURN TO EACH SECTION FOR INSIGHTS AND INSPIRATION:

VISIT THE SPRING SECTION WHEN:

- YOU ARE EXPERIENCING POSITIVE CHANGE
- YOU ARE UNDERGOING PERSONAL GROWTH
- YOU ARE CONSIDERING NEW IDEAS
- YOU ARE FEELING RESTLESS OR EXCITED
- YOU ARE OVERWHELMED BY ENERGY

VISIT THE SUMMER SECTION WHEN:

- YOU ARE FLOURISHING AND THRIVING
- YOU ARE CONTENT WITH WHERE YOU ARE
- YOU ARE EAGER TO TAKE ACTION
- YOU ARE FEELING BRAVE AND ALERT
- YOU ARE READY TO EXPLORE MORE

VISIT THE AUTUMN SECTION WHEN:

- YOU ARE FACING DIFFICULT CHALLENGES
- YOU ARE LONGING FOR TRANSFORMATION
- YOU ARE SEEKING BALANCE AND STABILITY
- YOU ARE IN NEED OF CONNECTION
- YOU ARE FEELING CONTEMPLATIVE

VISIT THE WINTER SECTION WHEN:

- YOU ARE IN NEED OF REST
- YOU ARE FEELING OVERWHELMED
- YOU ARE IN SEARCH OF SOLITUDE
- YOU ARE PLANNING FOR THE FUTURE
- YOU ARE ENTANGLED IN EMOTIONS

AS WITH REAL SEASONS, THERE ARE OVERLAPS IN EACH OF THESE, SO NOT EVERYTHING YOU EXPERIENCE CAN BE NEATLY PUT INTO ONE CATEGORY. THESE LISTS ARE MERELY A GUIDE TO GET YOU STARTED!

SPRING

SPRING IS...

... THE REMINDER THAT DELICATE SHOOTS MUST PUSH THROUGH DIRT

... THE REALIZATION OF HOW MUCH DARKNESS WE'VE SURVIVED

... THE TIME OF INDECISION, OF RESTLESS CLOUDS AND SOFT SUNSHINE

... THE KNOWLEDGE THAT NOT EVERYTHING BLOOMS AT THE SAME TIME

... THE ASTONISHMENT OF REGROWTH, OF THE FORGOTTEN REAWAKENING

... THE SEASON OF HOPE, OF TRYING BEFORE YOU KNOW YOU'LL SUCCEED

SPRING IS FILLED WITH MOVEMENT AND LIFE. EVERYTHING IS WAKING UP AFTER A LONG WINTER BREAK. THE SUN IS RISING HIGHER IN THE SKY, LEADING TO MORE WARMTH, STRENGTH, AND GROWTH.

AT THE BEGINNING OF THE SEASON, COLD SNAPS CAN OCCUR. JUST WHEN YOU THINK EVERYTHING IS WARM AND BRIGHT, THERE CAN BE SETBACKS. TRY TO TAKE SETBACKS IN STRIDE AND KNOW THAT, EVENTUALLY, THINGS WILL BEGIN TO BLOOM.

THIS SEASON IS THE TIME TO CONSUME NOURISHMENT FOR THE MONTHS TO COME. SOAK UP KNOWLEDGE AND ABSORB WHAT YOU CAN FROM EXPERIENCES NOW SO THAT YOU WILL HAVE STRENGTH TO KEEP FLOURISHING DURING THE HEAT OF SUMMER.

NOW IS THE SEASON TO APPRECIATE THE WAYS YOU'RE CHANGING AND SEEK TO ACCEPT HOW YOU FEEL ABOUT THOSE CHANGES WITHOUT JUDGMENT. IT IS ALSO THE TIME TO ACCEPT THE PACE AT WHICH YOU ARE GROWING. JUST AS YOU CANNOT FORCE A FLOWER TO BLOOM FASTER, YOU CANNOT FORCE YOURSELF TO GROW MORE QUICKLY.

EVERYTHING HAPPENS WHEN IT'S MEANT TO, AND THIS SEASON OF YOUR LIFE WILL HELP REMIND YOU OF THAT.

IT TAKES A LOT OF EFFORT
TO SEEK OUT THE SUN.

HAVING ROOTS
IN THE PAST DOESN'T
PREVENT A FRESH START.

EVEN WHEN IT'S POSITIVE, CHANGE CAN BE DIFFICULT BECAUSE IT REQUIRES GROWTH. YOU MAY EVEN GET EXACTLY WHAT YOU WANT (AND, LET'S BE REAL, THAT DOESN'T HAPPEN OFTEN), BUT IF CHANGE IS INVOLVED, YOU'RE GOING TO HAVE TO STRETCH YOURSELF IN NEW WAYS. ALLOW YOURSELF TO FEEL WHAT YOU FEEL DURING TIMES OF NEW GROWTH. THE MOST BEAUTIFUL TRANSFORMATIONS IN LIFE CAN ALSO BE PAINFUL.

IT'S OKAY TO
OUTGROW THOSE
WHO PREVENT YOU
FROM GROWING.

SURPRISINGLY,
LETTING GO IS
OFTEN EASIER THAN
HOLDING ON.

EVERY FLOWER OPENS
WHEN IT'S MEANT TO.

DID YOU KNOW THAT DIFFERENT
FLOWERS BLOOM AT DIFFERENT
TIMES OF THE DAY? SOME PREFER
MORNING, AND SPREAD THEIR
PETALS AS THE SUN RISES.
OTHERS OPEN UP IN THE EVENING.
PEOPLE ARE LIKE THAT, TOO. WE
ALL BLOOM AT DIFFERENT TIMES.
EVEN THOUGH IT MIGHT
SOMETIMES FEEL AS IF EVERYONE
IS FLOURISHING, REMEMBER TO
HAVE PATIENCE. WHEN YOU'RE
READY, YOU, TOO, WILL BLOOM.

VULNERABILITY
CAN BE A BRIDGE.

A LOT CAN BE HAPPENING BENEATH THE SURFACE.

TRANSFORMATION ISN'T ALWAYS VISIBLE. WHILE YOU MAY NOT SEE A CHANGE IN YOURSELF – OR IN OTHERS – YOU ARE STILL GROWING AND CHANGING EVERY DAY. IF YOU FIND YOURSELF FRUSTRATED WITH THE PACE OF CHANGE, TRY TO REMEMBER THAT A LOT CAN BE HAPPENING BENEATH THE SURFACE THAT YOU'RE NOT YET AWARE OF. IT'S OFTEN ONLY WHEN WE LOOK BACK AFTER A CHANGE THAT WE CAN SEE ALL OF THE LITTLE THINGS THAT HAD TO HAPPEN TO MAKE IT POSSIBLE.

WE'RE ALL JUST
DOING THE BEST WE
CAN WHERE WE ARE.

SETTING BOUNDARIES
IS AN ACT OF SELF-LOVE.

WE ALL NEED BOUNDARIES IN ORDER TO HAVE POSITIVE, PRODUCTIVE RELATIONSHIPS. IF YOU STRUGGLE TO SET BOUNDARIES, DON'T BE TOO HARD ON YOURSELF. IT CAN BE DIFFICULT TO RAISE A FENCE WHERE THERE WAS ONCE AN OPEN DOOR. DO YOUR BEST TO ESTABLISH THE LIMITS YOU NEED, LET OTHERS KNOW ABOUT THEM, AND DO NOT FEEL GUILTY FOR HAVING THEM. BOUNDARIES ARE NECESSARY AND IMPORTANT.

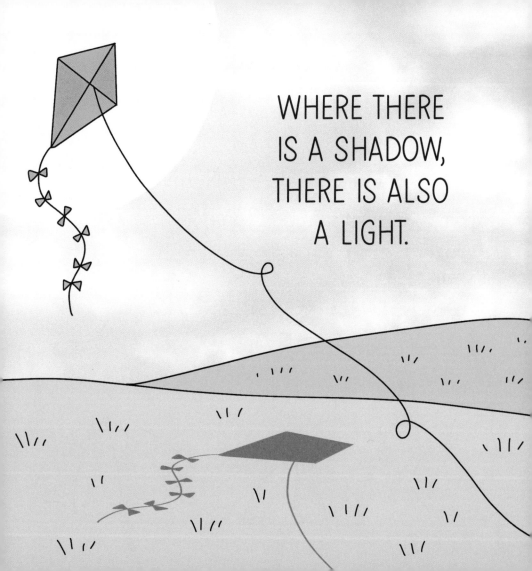

WHERE THERE
IS A SHADOW,
THERE IS ALSO
A LIGHT.

POSITIVITY ISN'T STANDING IN THE RAIN AND SAYING, "IT'S NOT RAINING." IT'S ABOUT FINDING THE SILVER LINING IN THE CLOUDS.

THERE IS A BIG DIFFERENCE BETWEEN HAPPINESS AND POSITIVITY. HAPPINESS IS A MOOD. IT IS FLEETING AND OFTEN OUT OF YOUR CONTROL. BUT POSITIVITY IS A MIND-SET – A LOGICAL TACTIC THAT CAN BE LEARNED. ONCE YOU DISCOVER THAT YOU CAN'T ALWAYS BE HAPPY BUT YOU CAN ALWAYS BE POSITIVE, IT BECOMES A LOT EASIER TO DEAL WITH LIFE'S STORMS.

IF YOU LOOK CLOSELY,
YOU CAN FIND INSPIRATION
ALMOST ANYWHERE.

STOP LOOKING
FOR THE POT
OF GOLD
AND, INSTEAD,
APPRECIATE
THE RAINBOW.

THE DIFFERENCE
BETWEEN A
WEED AND A
FLOWER IS ALL
IN HOW WE
NAME IT.

THE WORDS YOU USE TO DEFINE YOURSELF AND THE THINGS, PEOPLE, AND EXPERIENCES SURROUNDING YOU HAVE A MASSIVE IMPACT ON HOW YOU PERCEIVE THE WORLD. LABELS, LIKE IT OR NOT, HAVE AN INFLUENCE ON WHAT A THING BECOMES. TRY TO KEEP THAT IN MIND WHEN CHOOSING WORDS – PARTICULARLY WORDS THAT FOLLOW THE PHRASE "I AM..."

EVERYTHING
NEEDS HELP
TO GROW.

YOU NEED THE RAIN IF YOU WANT THE STRENGTH TO STRETCH UP TO THE SUN.

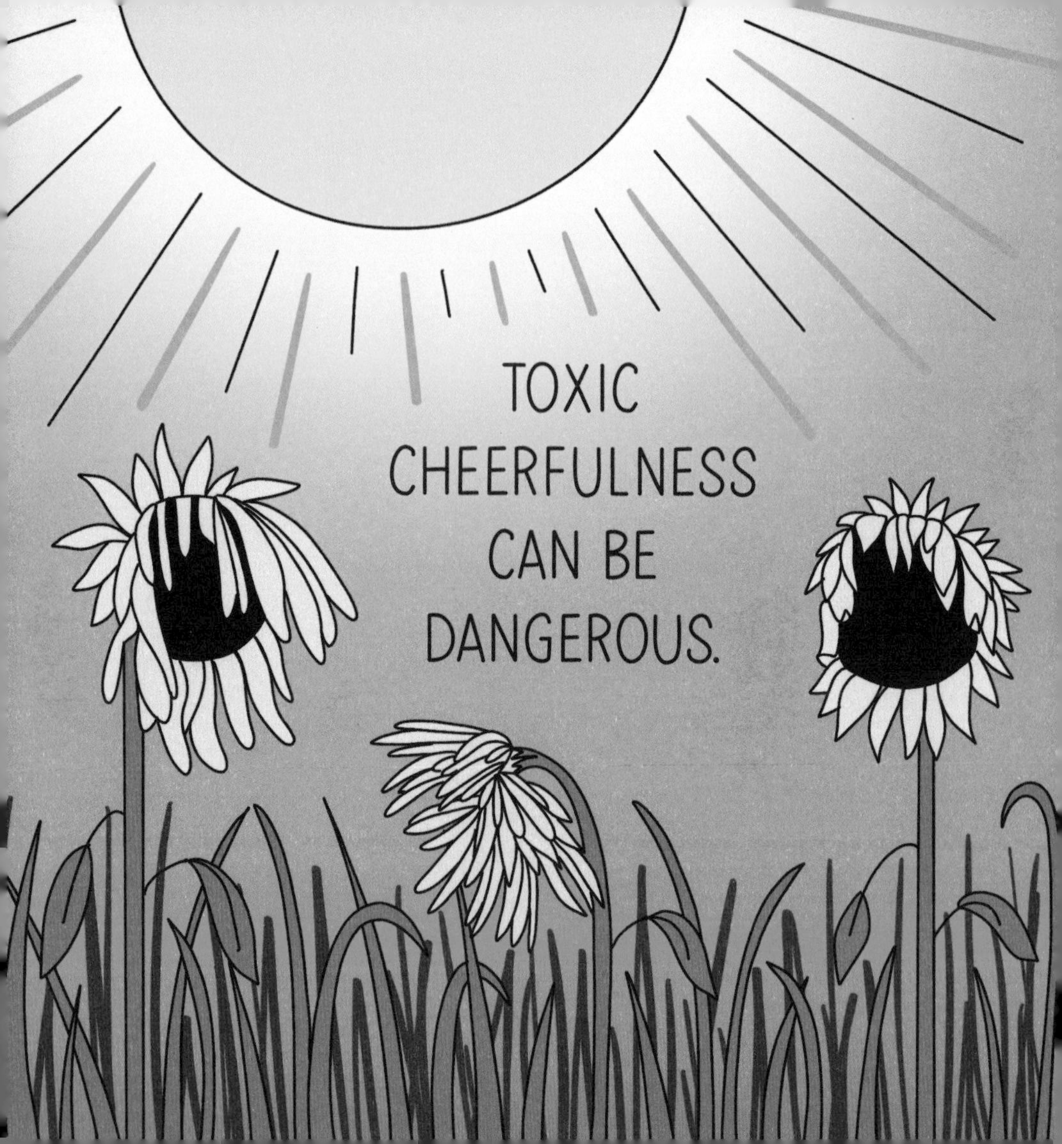
TOXIC CHEERFULNESS CAN BE DANGEROUS.

TOXIC CHEERFULNESS IS THE IDEA THAT PUTTING ON A HAPPY FACE AND MUSCLING THROUGH A BAD PATCH WILL MAKE EVERYTHING OKAY. WHILE IT'S LOVELY TO BE UPBEAT, BEING OPTIMISTIC DOESN'T MEAN IGNORING PAIN OR TRYING TO DROWN IT IN CHEER. IT'S OKAY TO HAVE "NEGATIVE" EMOTIONS. IT'S OKAY TO HAVE TOUGH TIMES AND BAD DAYS. LET YOURSELF FEEL THEM, AND DON'T THINK YOU NEED TO SMILE THROUGH IT ALL.

PAUSE AND PONDER THE DAISIES.

SOMETIMES YOU NEED
A STORM TO CLEAR THE AIR.

YOUR LIFE IS FILLED WITH MANY DIFFERENT CHAPTERS – SOME WONDERFUL, SOME NOT SO GREAT – AND HOW YOU TELL (AND THINK ABOUT) THOSE STORIES MATTERS. YOU CANNOT CHANGE THE PAST, BUT YOU CAN REFRAME IT, FOR BETTER OR WORSE! YOU HAVE THE POWER TO TELL YOUR STORIES YOUR OWN WAY, AND IT'S WORTH PAUSING TO CONSIDER IF THE WAY YOU TELL THEM IS BENEFICIAL FOR YOU.

REFRESH YOUR
SURROUNDINGS,
REFRESH YOUR
MIND-SET.

THERE'S A
DIFFERENCE BETWEEN
PLANNING AND WORRYING.

IF YOU'RE A PLAN-AHEAD TYPE, YOU KNOW THERE'S A FINE LINE BETWEEN BEING PREPARED AND WORRYING ABOUT EVERYTHING THAT COULD POSSIBLY GO WRONG. TRY TO BE GENTLE WITH YOURSELF AND REMEMBER THAT, LIKE IT OR NOT, LIFE IS FILLED WITH THINGS WE CANNOT PREPARE FOR. DO YOUR BEST TO BE READY FOR WHAT COMES, BUT REMIND YOURSELF THAT YOU DON'T HAVE TO BE READY FOR EVERYTHING.

SPRING WISHLIST

PATIENCE: CULTIVATE A WILLINGNESS TO WAIT AND ENDURE WHATEVER CHANGES COME YOUR WAY.

FOCUS: KEEP YOUR GOALS IN MIND, EVEN WHEN IT'S EASY TO BE DISTRACTED BY EVERYTHING TRANSFORMING AROUND YOU.

ENERGY: BUILD UP YOUR STRENGTH AND REMEMBER THAT GROWTH CAN BE A TOUGH PROCESS, EVEN WHEN IT'S BENEFICIAL.

SUMMER

SUMMER IS...

... THE TIME TO SLOW DOWN AND TAKE IN
THE WORLD AROUND YOU

... THE REMINDER OF SUN-SOAKED
CONNECTION TO INNOCENCE

... THE KNOWLEDGE THAT FREEDOM IS
BOTH A BLESSING AND A CURSE

... THE REALIZATION THAT, YES, MOST OF
THE SEEDS PLANTED WILL FLOURISH

... THE CONNECTION TO ADVENTURE (EVEN
IF IT'S JUST IN YOUR OWN BACKYARD)

... THE SEASON OF LIGHT, OF ILLUMINATING
THE TRUTH OF WHO YOU ARE

A SUMMER SEASON IS VIBRANT AND EXCITING. IN THIS SEASON, MUCH OF THE DIFFICULTY OF NEW GROWTH IS OVERCOME, AND NOW IS THE TIME FOR YOU TO EXPAND ON WHAT WAS BEGUN IN THE LAST SEASON.

BLOOMING AND GROWING TOOK A LOT OF EFFORT, AND WHILE THINGS WILL CONTINUE TO THRIVE IN THIS SEASON, THIS IS ALSO A TIME THAT INVOLVES A MIX OF RELAXATION AND ACTION.

IN SUMMER, PLANS WILL COME TO FRUITION, AND THERE WILL BE MORE GROWTH. THIS IS YOUR TIME FOR EXPANSION AND CREATION. IT IS ALSO THE SEASON OF ABUNDANCE AND SUCCESS.

EVEN IN THE SUNNIEST OF TIMES, THERE CAN BE STORMS. NO SEASON IS WITHOUT DIFFICULTY, BUT THE STORMS THAT COME HAVE A PURPOSE. THEY WILL PROVIDE NOURISHMENT AND STRENGTH.

IF YOU ALLOW IT, THERE CAN BE LUXURIOUSLY LAZY MOMENTS IN THIS SEASON. LEARN TO REST WITHOUT GROWING RESTLESS. AS YOU MOVE THROUGH IT, REMEMBER THAT SUMMER'S LIGHT ALWAYS DIMS AT SOME POINT. ENJOY THE TIMES IN WHICH YOU ARE THRIVING.

PLANT
WHAT YOU
WOULD
LIKE TO SEE
GROW.

IF YOU WANT TREASURE,
YOU HAVE TO SEARCH FOR IT.

MORE FREEDOM
ISN'T ALWAYS
LIBERATING.

WITH MORE HOURS OF DAYLIGHT EACH DAY, SUMMER FEELS LIBERATING IN A WAY THAT OTHER SEASONS DO NOT. BUT FREEDOM – AND TIME – IS A DOUBLE-EDGED SWORD. IF YOU DON'T HAVE ENOUGH OF IT, YOU FEEL CONSTRICTED AND STRESSED. TOO MUCH OF IT AND YOU FEEL RESTLESS AND OVERWHELMED. TRY TO FIND A BALANCE BETWEEN FLYING FREE AND KEEPING YOUR FEET ON THE GROUND.

GIVE THINGS IN YOUR LIFE TIME TO RIPEN.

THERE ARE TIMES WHEN THE PATH IS CLEAR, AND THERE ARE TIMES YOU HAVE NO IDEA WHAT'S GOING TO HAPPEN NEXT.

REGARDLESS OF WHETHER OR NOT YOUR PATH APPEARS CLEARLY BEFORE YOU, KNOW THAT YOU'RE NOT ALONE. IF YOUR PATH IS CLEAR AND WELL-MARKED, FOLLOW IT WITH CONFIDENCE. IF YOU'RE UNSURE OF WHICH WAY TO GO, WEIGH YOUR OPTIONS THE BEST THAT YOU CAN, MAKE A CHOICE, AND SET OFF. WHATEVER YOU CHOOSE WILL LEAD YOU TO WHERE YOU ARE MEANT TO GO.

THE TINIEST GLOW CAN
BRIGHTEN THE DARKNESS.

DAYDREAMING CAN BE
THE START OF DAY-DOING.

BE THANKFUL FOR THE TIMES
WHEN YOU'RE THRIVING.

ODDLY ENOUGH, IT CAN BE A CHALLENGE TO BE GRATEFUL FOR GOOD DAYS IN YOUR LIFE (PARTICULARLY IF YOU'VE HAD A LOT OF BAD ONES). WHEN A GOOD DAY COMES YOUR WAY, DO YOUR BEST TO EMBRACE IT WITHOUT FEELING GUILTY OR WORRYING ABOUT WHEN THE GOOD TIMES WILL END. TRY YOUR HARDEST TO ENJOY (AND BE FULLY PRESENT IN) THE TIMES IN WHICH YOU ARE FLOURISHING.

THERE IS NEVER A "PERFECT" MOMENT. DON'T WAIT.

NEVER BE AFRAID TO PUT WHAT YOU WANT OUT INTO THE WORLD.

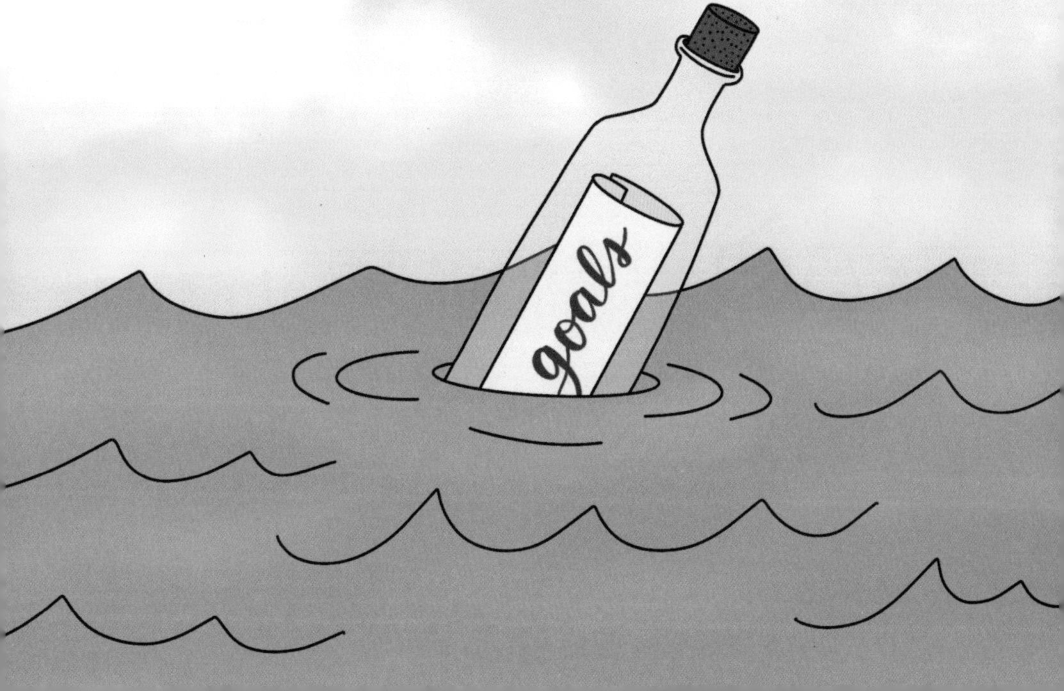

YOU MAY WANT TO SET SOME THINGS DOWN.

YOU'RE NOT ALONE IF YOU CARRY AROUND THINGS THAT AREN'T HELPFUL TO YOU, WHETHER THAT'S EMOTIONS ABOUT THE PAST, REGRETS, OR NEGATIVE RELATIONSHIPS. YOU MAY NOT BE ABLE TO SET ALL THAT WEIGHT DOWN NOW, BUT THAT DOESN'T MEAN YOU WILL CARRY IT FOREVER. BE PATIENT. LET GO OF WHAT YOU CAN, AND ACCEPT WHAT YOU MUST HOLD ON TO FOR NOW.

NEVER FORGET:
A PEARL STARTS OUT AS A
SINGLE GRAIN OF SAND.

IT DOESN'T HAVE TO BE
A HOME RUN TO COUNT
AS POSITIVE PROGRESS.

YOUR WORLD IS TINTED BY THE LENS YOU'RE LOOKING THROUGH.

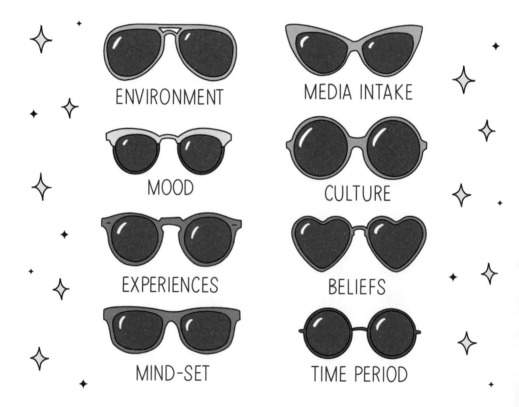

ENVIRONMENT

MEDIA INTAKE

MOOD

CULTURE

EXPERIENCES

BELIEFS

MIND-SET

TIME PERIOD

EVERY PERSON HAS A COMPLETELY UNIQUE POINT OF VIEW. YOUR PERSPECTIVE (LITERALLY AND FIGURATIVELY), YOUR EXPERIENCES, YOUR CULTURE, YOUR MIND-SET, AND A MILLION OTHER LITTLE THINGS COME TOGETHER TO TINT YOUR VIEW OF THE WORLD. IT'S WORTH REFLECTING ON WHAT LENSES YOU MIGHT BE LOOKING THROUGH.

WHEN SEAS ARE STORMY, DON'T BE AFRAID TO LOOK FOR GUIDANCE.

YOU WON'T
FEEL THIS WAY
FOREVER.

JUST BECAUSE EVERYONE
ELSE IS ENJOYING IT
DOESN'T MEAN
YOU HAVE TO.

THERE MAY BE TIMES WHEN YOU EXPECT TO FEEL HAPPY, BUT YOU END UP FEELING CONFUSED OR DISAPPOINTED THAT YOU'RE NOT AS JOYFUL AS YOU'D HOPED. JUST BECAUSE A SITUATION IS EXPECTED TO BE A HAPPY ONE DOESN'T MEAN YOU'LL NECESSARILY FEEL THAT WAY. ALLOW YOURSELF TO FEEL HOW YOU FEEL, AND DON'T FEEL GUILTY IF YOUR EMOTIONS DON'T ALWAYS ALIGN PERFECTLY WITH YOUR EXPECTATIONS.

THERE'S NOTHING WRONG WITH TAKING A BREAK FROM THE CROWD.

ENCOURAGE
YOUR IMAGINATION.

EVEN IF YOU DON'T CONSIDER YOURSELF A CREATIVE PERSON (IN FACT, ESPECIALLY IF YOU DON'T CONSIDER YOURSELF A CREATIVE PERSON), MAKING TIME FOR IMAGINATION AND EXPLORING A CREATIVE PURSUIT IS WORTHWHILE. TAKE TIME TO PLAY, TO MAKE, TO BE SILLY. TAKE TIME TO LOOK AT CLOUDS AND WISH ON STARS AND IMAGINE RIDICULOUS THINGS. IT MIGHT SEEM FRIVOLOUS, BUT IT'S ONE OF THE MOST PRODUCTIVE THINGS YOU CAN DO.

WE ALL THRIVE
WHEN WE'RE IN THE
RIGHT ENVIRONMENT.

SOME OF US HAVE
TO SWIM HARDER TO
KEEP OUR HEADS
ABOVE WATER.

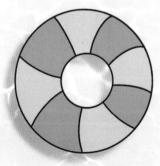

WHAT WOULD IT
BE LIKE TO SPEND
MORE TIME STROLLING
THAN YOU DO SCROLLING?

FOR MOST OF US, SCROLLING IS PART OF LIFE THESE DAYS, BUT IT DOESN'T HAVE TO BE YOUR WHOLE LIFE. TAKE A BREAK FROM TECH AND LET YOURSELF EXPLORE THE WORLD AROUND YOU WITHOUT LOOKING UP THE WHY AND HOW AND WHO OF IT ALL. YOU CAN LEARN JUST AS MUCH FROM LIVING AS YOU CAN FROM SEARCHING.

YOU GROW STRONGER
WITH EVERY SINGLE
STORM YOU WEATHER.

DON'T SHRINK
YOURSELF DOWN
TO MAKE SOMEONE
ELSE FEEL BIG.

THE MORE YOU
OPEN YOUR MIND,
THE MORE YOU'LL
BE ABLE TO FIND.

OPENING YOUR MIND CAN CHANGE YOUR WHOLE LIFE. IT WILL HELP YOU CREATE OPPORTUNITIES WHERE THERE SEEMED TO BE NONE. IT WILL HELP YOU UNDERSTAND OTHERS (AND YOURSELF) BETTER. IT WILL HELP YOU GROW AND EXPLORE IN WAYS YOU HADN'T CONSIDERED BEFORE. EVEN IF YOU THINK YOU HAVE AN OPEN MIND, TRY YOUR BEST TO OPEN IT EVEN WIDER.

AUTUMN

AUTUMN IS...

... THE TIME TO GATHER KNOWLEDGE AND HARVEST NEW IDEAS

... THE PAUSE NEEDED TO EMBRACE TRUE, INSPIRING GRATITUDE

... THE KNOWLEDGE THAT THERE IS BOTH PAIN AND FREEDOM IN LETTING GO

... THE REMINDER THAT SOMETIMES PATIENCE IS WHAT LEADS TO GROWTH

... THE ACCEPTANCE OF OUR OWN MATCHLESS, MAGNIFICENT MAGIC

... THE SEASON OF CONTRAST, OF HOLDING ON AND LETTING GO

THE AUTUMN SEASON IS ABOUT SLOWING DOWN AND TAKING TIME TO THOUGHTFULLY GATHER KNOWLEDGE AND INSPIRATION FOR THE FUTURE.

WHAT YOU PLANTED EARLIER IN THE YEAR IS NOW RIPE AND READY. IT IS THE SEASON OF ENJOYING HARD WORK PAYING OFF, AS WELL AS MAKING SURE YOU PREPARE FOR THE TIMES WHEN YOUR BOUNTY WON'T BE AS PLENTIFUL.

IN AUTUMN, YOU'RE GATHERING THE FRUITS OF YOUR LABOR, BUT YOU'RE ALSO GETTING RID OF WHAT MIGHT WEIGH YOU DOWN. TREES SHED THEIR LEAVES IN AUTUMN SO WINTER SNOWS WON'T BREAK THEIR BRANCHES. YOU, TOO, HAVE TO LET GO OF SOME THINGS TO MAKE SURE THAT YOU CAN THRIVE.

THIS IS A SEASON OF EMBRACING THE ARRIVAL OF WHAT YOU'VE WORKED HARD ON IN PREVIOUS SEASONS, AS WELL AS PAYING ATTENTION TO (AND PREPARING FOR) WHAT'S TO COME.

IN THE SLOWING DOWN, IN THE DARKENING OF EACH DAY, YOU CAN CHOOSE TO APPRECIATE THE BALANCE OF DARKNESS AND LIGHT, THE BRIDGE BETWEEN SUMMER'S CHAOTIC COLORS AND WINTER'S SLOW STILLNESS.

CELEBRATE
HOW FAR
YOU'VE
COME.

SELF-LOVE

ACCEPTANCE

A LOT GOES
INTO HAVING AN
OPTIMISTIC OUTLOOK.

INSPIRATION

GRATITUDE

OPEN-
MINDEDNESS

CREATE MORE OPTIMISM BY FOCUSING ON A FEW KEY INGREDIENTS, INCLUDING:

- GRATITUDE: APPRECIATING WHAT YOU HAVE MAKES IT EASIER TO SEE THE GOOD.
- SELF-LOVE: FINDING THE GOOD IN YOURSELF IS THE BEGINNING OF FINDING THE GOOD EVERYWHERE.
- ACCEPTANCE: ADMITTING WHAT YOU CAN AND CANNOT CHANGE IS LIBERATING.
- OPEN-MINDEDNESS: DISCOVERING THAT OPPORTUNITY CAN BE FOUND ANYWHERE MAKES OPTIMISM EASIER.
- INSPIRATION: FINDING INSPIRATION MOTIVATES YOU TO KEEP SEEKING OUT LIFE'S GOOD.

DO WHAT YOU CAN
TO AVOID GETTING
TANGLED IN NEGATIVITY.

IF YOU SPEND YOUR TIME LOOKING TO THE FUTURE, YOU'LL LOSE SIGHT OF THE PRESENT.

WHILE IT'S USEFUL TO PLAN FOR WHAT'S TO COME (AND HAVE THINGS TO LOOK FORWARD TO!), IF YOU SPEND ALL OF YOUR TIME THINKING ABOUT WHAT YOU'RE GOING TO DO SOMEDAY, YOU'RE MISSING OUT ON WHAT'S HAPPENING TODAY. REMAINING IN THE MOMENT CAN BE DIFFICULT. TRY TO REMIND YOURSELF YOU HAVE TO SPEND TIME IN THE PRESENT BEFORE THE FUTURE BECOMES A REALITY.

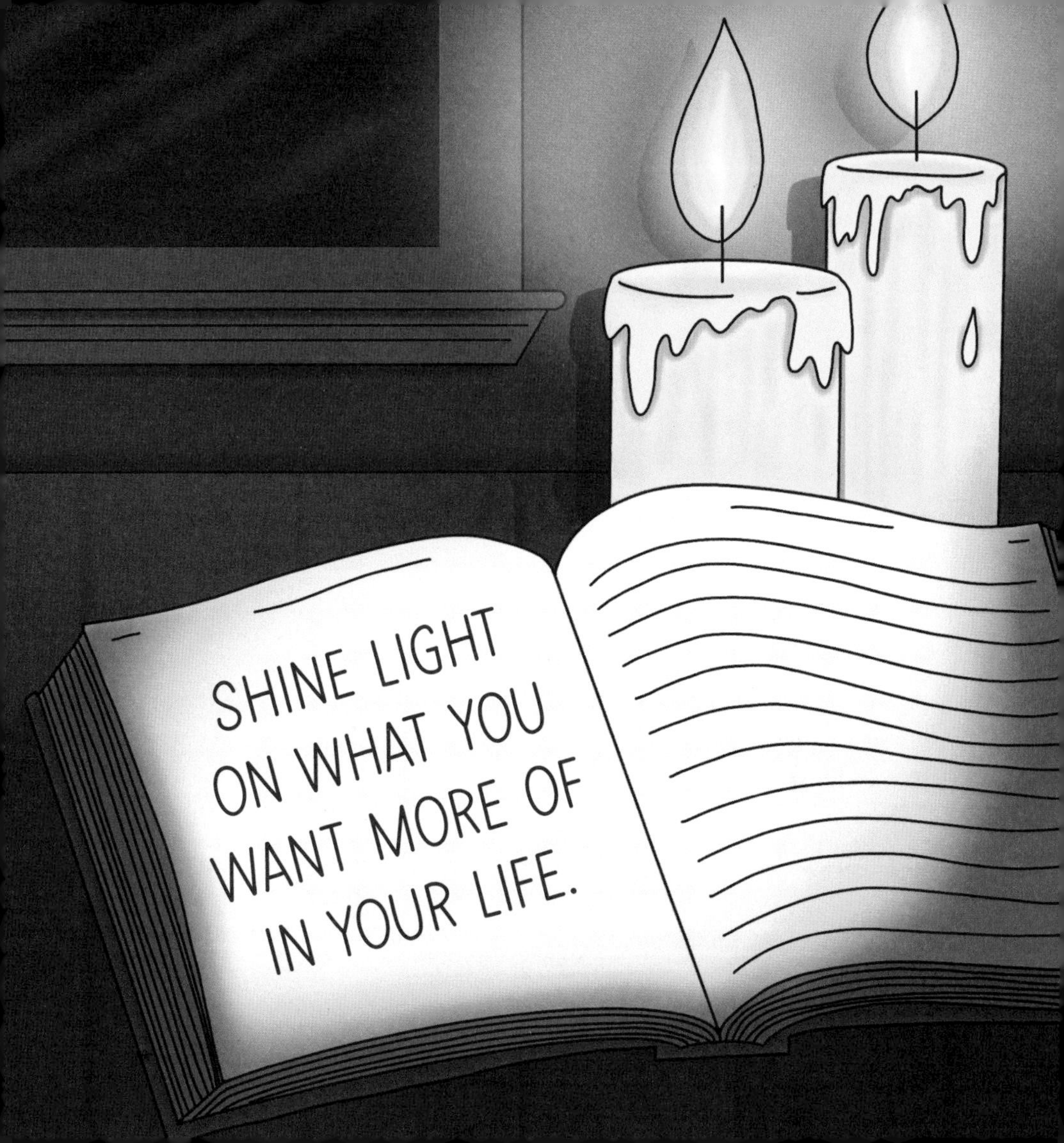
SHINE LIGHT
ON WHAT YOU
WANT MORE OF
IN YOUR LIFE.

GRATITUDE BRIGHTENS
EVEN THE DARKEST
OF TIMES.

TRUE GRATITUDE COMES FROM NOT JUST REFLECTING ON WHAT YOU HAVE TO BE THANKFUL FOR BUT FROM TAKING NOTICE OF IT IN REAL TIME. NO MATTER WHERE YOU ARE IN YOUR LIFE — IN YOUR BEST SEASON OR YOUR WORST — PAYING ATTENTION TO WHAT'S GOING WELL (EVEN THE TINIEST OF THINGS) WILL ADD STARLIGHT TO YOUR NIGHT SKY.

A SCAR CAN BE
A REMINDER OF HOW
MUCH YOU'VE BEEN
HURT – OR OF HOW
MUCH YOU'VE
HEALED.

YOU ARE ALLOWED TO FEEL - AND
EXPRESS! - YOUR EMOTIONS.

ABCDEFGHIJKLMNOPQRSTUVWXYZ

APPRECIATE HOW
MANY QUESTIONS YOU'VE
ALREADY ANSWERED.

SO MUCH OF LIFE IS A MYSTERY. TAKE A MOMENT TO THINK OF HOW MUCH YOU'VE LEARNED SO FAR, AND YOU'LL BE IMPRESSED WITH YOURSELF. EVEN IN THE PAST YEAR, YOU'VE PICKED UP ALL KINDS OF KNOWLEDGE THAT YOU DIDN'T HAVE BEFORE. YES, THERE IS MUCH THAT'S UNKNOWN, BUT DON'T LET UNCERTAINTIES PREVENT YOU FROM BEING AWED BY ALL THAT YOU NOW UNDERSTAND.

BEHIND EVERY
CLOUDY SKY,
THERE ARE STILL
STARS SHINING.

WHAT
YOU'RE
HOLDING
ON TO
MIGHT BE
WHAT'S
HOLDING
YOU BACK.

WHAT YOU REALLY "NEED" IN YOUR LIFE IS VERY DIFFERENT FROM WHAT YOU "WANT." DEEP DOWN, YOU KNOW WHAT'S BEST FOR YOU, AND IF THERE'S SOMETHING TELLING YOU TO LET GO, LISTEN TO THAT INSTINCT. BE INSPIRED BY AUTUMN'S TREES AND RELEASE WHAT IS WEIGHING YOU DOWN SO THAT, WHEN YOU'RE READY, YOU'LL HAVE ROOM FOR SOMETHING NEW.

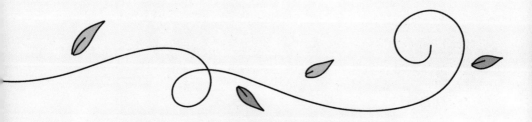

IT'S OKAY TO MAKE A MESS. IT'S HOW YOU FIND OUT WHO YOU ARE.

WHILE WE ALL REQUIRE THE BASICS — AIR, WATER, FOOD, SHELTER, LOVE — WE EACH HAVE VERY UNIQUE NEEDS WHEN IT COMES TO THE ENVIRONMENTS IN WHICH WE FLOURISH. THE MORE YOU PAY ATTENTION TO HOW YOU FEEL IN CERTAIN SITUATIONS, THE MORE YOU'LL BEGIN TO RECOGNIZE THE ENVIRONMENTS THAT HELP YOU TO GROW. YOU CAN STRIVE TO SURROUND YOURSELF WITH THESE CONDITIONS AS MUCH AS POSSIBLE.

SELF-AWARENESS
IS A KIND OF MAGIC.

compassion

balance

understanding

YOU DESERVE
TO WRAP YOURSELF
IN THE WARMTH YOU
GIVE TO OTHERS.

FEAR WILL HAUNT
YOU. LEARN TO WALK
THROUGH IT, NOT
AROUND IT.

FEAR IS A VERY NORMAL PART OF
BEING ALIVE, BUT IF YOU WANT TO
MAKE IT EASIER TO BEAR, TRY TO
FACE IT RATHER THAN RUN FROM IT.
NOT ONLY WILL YOU LIKELY
OVERCOME YOUR FEAR (THINGS ARE
OFTEN A LOT WORSE IN YOUR HEAD
THAN IN REALITY), BUT YOU'LL
COME THROUGH IT A STRONGER,
BRAVER PERSON. IF YOU'RE NOT
READY YET, THAT'S OKAY. BUT DO
YOUR BEST TO BE OPEN TO THE IDEA
THAT YOU – YES, YOU! – ARE
BRAVER THAN YOU REALIZE.

YOU CAN OFTEN CHOOSE TO
WALK AWAY FROM WHAT'S
NO GOOD FOR YOU.

SOME THINGS NEED
TO BE UNLEARNED.

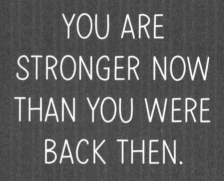

YOU ARE
STRONGER NOW
THAN YOU WERE
BACK THEN.

FOR BETTER OR WORSE, WHAT WE
EXPERIENCE AS CHILDREN OFTEN STICKS
WITH US LONG INTO ADULTHOOD. IT CAN
BE DIFFICULT TO MOVE BEYOND THE PAST,
BUT YOU HAVE THE POWER TO CHOOSE
WHAT YOU FOCUS ON TODAY. YES, THERE
WILL BE ECHOES OF WHAT WAS, BUT YOU
ARE STRONG AND BRAVE AND CAPABLE,
AND YOU HAVE THE POWER TO WALK
OUT OF THE PAST AND INTO THE PRESENT.

PAY ATTENTION TO
WHAT YOU SEE IN YOUR
DARK MOMENTS.

RELAXING MIGHT FEEL AS IF YOU ARE DOING NOTHING, BUT SLOWING DOWN IS NOT THE SAME AS STOPPING. HARD AS IT IS TO BELIEVE IN OUR FAST-PACED WORLD, LIFE IS NOT ACTUALLY MEANT TO BE A NEVER-ENDING HARVEST. LIKE THE EARTH, WE, TOO, NEED TIME TO RESTORE AND REPLENISH OUR RESOURCES. RESTING IS ITS OWN KIND OF HARD WORK, AND JUST BECAUSE YOU DON'T SEE THE RESULTS DOESN'T MEAN NOTHING'S HAPPENING.

AUTUMN WISHLIST

COURAGE: FIND INNER STRENGTH DURING THE DARK MOMENTS OF THE SEASON.

GRATITUDE: IDENTIFY WHAT YOU ARE FORTUNATE ENOUGH TO POSSESS AND EXPERIENCE (YES, EVEN TOUGH STUFF!).

ACCEPTANCE: ACKNOWLEDGE WHAT YOU SEE BEFORE YOU AND CHOOSE TO EMBRACE IT.

WINTER

WINTER IS...

... THE TIME TO REFLECT ON WHAT HAS HAPPENED AND WHAT'S TO COME

... THE UNDERSTANDING THAT SILENCE POSSESSES A KIND OF WISDOM

... THE BRIDGE BETWEEN LETTING GO AND EMBRACING GROWTH

... THE KNOWLEDGE THAT SLOWING DOWN IS NECESSARY

... THE BELIEF THAT EVEN THE DARKEST OF TIMES WILL PASS

... THE SEASON OF REST, OF MAKING ROOM FOR WHAT WILL COME

THE WINTER SEASON IS A TIME OF SLOWNESS AND STILLNESS. MUCH OF NATURE IS AT REST DURING THIS TIME, PREPARING FOR THE LIVELY SEASONS TO COME.

THERE ARE TIMES WHEN YOU ARE REQUIRED TO SLOW DOWN, EVEN IF IT'S DIFFICULT FOR YOU. JUST AS FROST REMINDS PLANTS TO REST, YOU MIGHT HAVE SOMETHING THAT IS SLOWING YOUR GROWTH IN THIS PARTICULAR SEASON. THIS SLOWER TIME OF LIFE MAY BE CHALLENGING FOR YOU, BUT NOT ALL SEASONS ARE ABOUT GROWTH.

YOUR WORTH IS NOT MEASURED BY HOW PRODUCTIVE YOU ARE. TAKING TIME TO REST, REFLECT, AND RECOVER IS WHAT WINTER IS ALL ABOUT.

THIS IS THE SEASON TO PRACTICE PATIENCE, TO BUILD ON THE LESSONS OF ACCEPTANCE THAT YOU DISCOVERED IN AUTUMN. THE WORLD MIGHT SEEM COLD AND BARE, BUT WITH A CHILL COMES CLARITY THAT ISN'T AVAILABLE IN OTHER SEASONS.

THERE MAY BE MORE DARKNESS IN YOUR WINTER, BUT IT'S IN THE DARKNESS THAT LIGHTS SHINE BRIGHTEST.

JUST BECAUSE
IT'S FROZEN NOW
DOESN'T MEAN IT
WON'T THAW
SOMEDAY.

PAY MORE ATTENTION TO WHAT YOU ALREADY HAVE.

IN TIMES OF DARKNESS, IT'S IMPORTANT TO CREATE YOUR OWN COMFORT. WHAT THIS COMFORT LOOKS LIKE WILL BE DIFFERENT FOR EVERYONE – SOME MIGHT FIND CONTENTMENT IN OTHERS; SOME MIGHT SEEK SOLACE IN SOLITUDE. IN ANY CASE, WHEN LIFE FEELS DARK, SHOW YOURSELF THE SAME COMPASSION YOU'D SHOW OTHERS AND SEEK OUT WHAT BRINGS YOU COMFORT.

THE SOONER YOU LET YOUR FEELINGS IN, THE SOONER THEY'LL LEAVE.

FEELINGS COME AND GO LIKE THE WEATHER. INSTEAD OF CLOSING YOURSELF OFF FROM THEM, CONSIDER LETTING THEM IN TO STAY FOR A WHILE — EVEN WHEN THEY'RE DIFFICULT. SURE, IT MIGHT GET A LITTLE MESSY, AND JUST LIKE BAD WEATHER, THEY SOMETIMES STICK AROUND LONGER THAN YOU'D LIKE. BUT EVENTUALLY THEY WILL PASS (OR MELT!), AND YOUR WORLD WILL BE CALMER ONCE AGAIN.

THE JOURNEY DOESN'T END WHEN YOU HIT AN OBSTACLE.

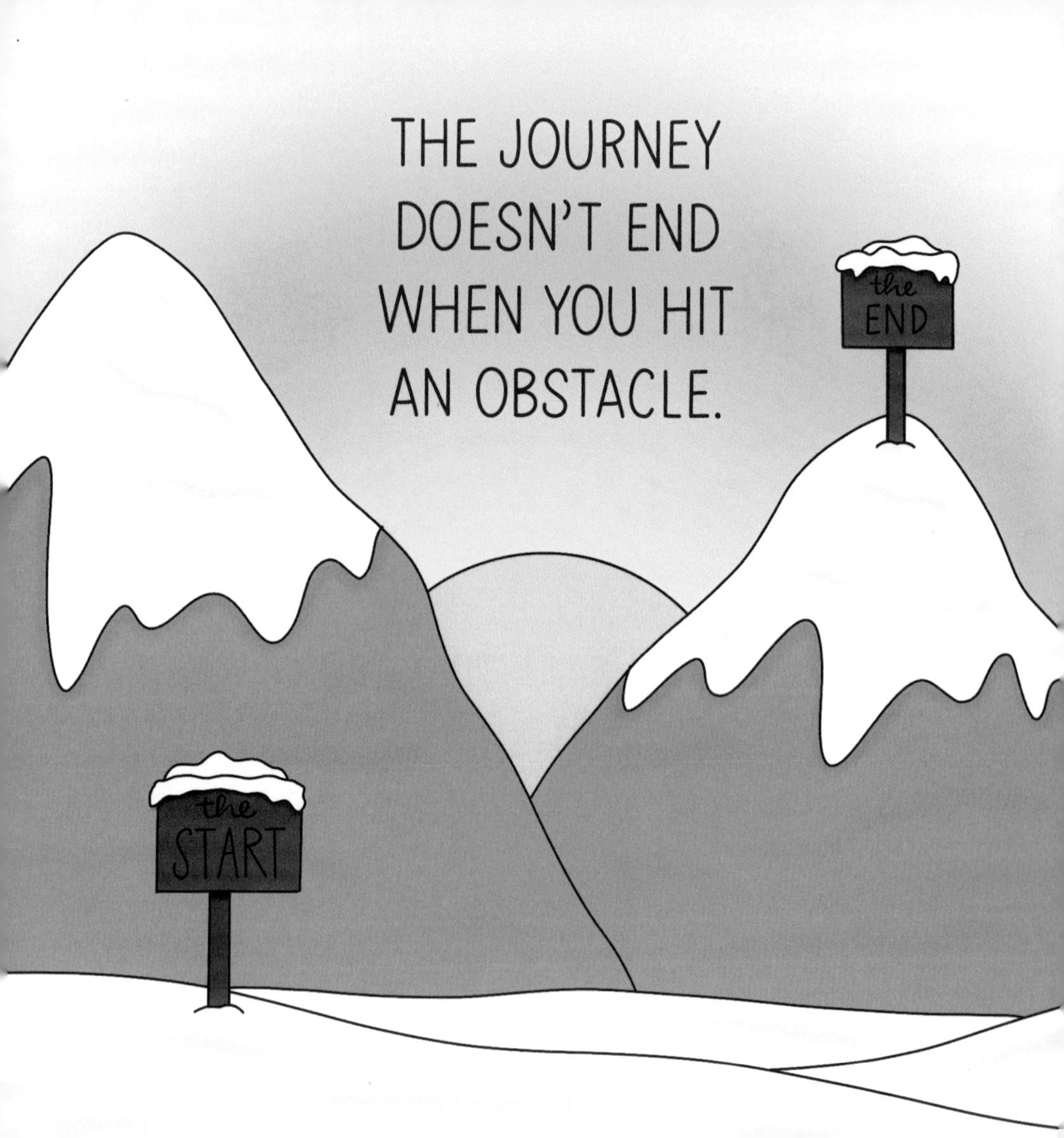

FIND THE MAGIC IN THE MUNDANE.

MENU

travel-the-world tea

♥

marriage macchiato

♥

education espresso

♥

café creative life

career-change cappuccino

♥

buy-a-home brew

♥

lots-of-little-ones latte

♥

more-money mocha

IT'S OKAY IF YOU'RE UNSURE ABOUT WHAT TO CHOOSE.

SOMETIMES LIFE FEELS LIKE IT'S JUST CHOICE AFTER CHOICE AFTER CHOICE, AND WHEN IT COMES TO THE BIG ONES, IT CAN LEAVE YOU FEELING DREADFULLY OVERWHELMED. WHEN THIS HAPPENS, REMIND YOURSELF THAT WHATEVER CHOICE YOU MAKE IS THE RIGHT ONE. WHATEVER PATH YOU TAKE IS NOW YOUR PATH. IT'S NORMAL TO BE UNCERTAIN, BUT YOU NEVER KNOW WHAT THE FUTURE WILL HOLD, SO EMBRACE WHATEVER YOU'VE CHOSEN.

APPRECIATE CONTRASTS.
IN EVERYTHING, THERE
IS A BRIGHT SPOT.

LOOK FOR THE
BEAUTY IN
EVERY SEASON.

THE MORE YOU LOOK FOR BEAUTY, THE MORE YOU WILL FIND IT – IT MIGHT JUST TAKE A LITTLE BIT OF PRACTICE. THE MORE TIME YOU SPEND LOOKING FOR IT, THE EASIER IT BECOMES. REGARDLESS OF WHERE YOU ARE, RIGHT IN THIS MOMENT, THERE IS SOMETHING BEAUTIFUL NEARBY. SEEK IT OUT.

SOMETIMES YOU HAVE TO
SHAKE THINGS UP AND
SEE WHAT HAPPENS.

THE PATH
YOU'RE ON IS
THE RIGHT ONE.

ACCEPTING WHERE YOU ARE, EVEN IF IT'S NOT WHERE YOU WANT TO BE, IS ONE OF THE BEST THINGS YOU CAN DO FOR YOURSELF. CONSIDER HOW FAR YOU'VE COME SINCE THE DAY YOU WERE BORN. SO MANY THINGS HAVE HAPPENED THAT YOU COULD NEVER HAVE PREDICTED (MANY OF WHICH WERE OUT OF YOUR CONTROL). YOU DON'T KNOW WHERE THIS PATH WILL LEAD, BUT TRUST THAT IT'S THE RIGHT ONE.

SOMETIMES
YOU HAVE TO
SUBTRACT
SOME THINGS
TO MAKE YOUR
LIFE ADD UP.

SET ASIDE TIME FOR
POSITIVE PURSUITS.

NOT A SINGLE ONE OF US IS A FINISHED PRODUCT. EVERY DAY, EVERY MOMENT, IS A CHANCE TO GROW, CHANGE, AND EXPLORE NEW WAYS OF BEING AND THINKING. YES, YOU MIGHT WISH YOU WERE IN A DIFFERENT STAGE, BUT KNOW THAT YOU'RE NOT ALONE IN THIS. WANTING TO GROW IS A GOOD THING, BUT RECOGNIZING THAT IT'S OKAY TO BE IN THE PROCESS OF BECOMING IS JUST AS IMPORTANT.

MOST PEOPLE HAVE MORE
GOING ON THAN YOU CAN SEE.

BE WILLING
TO OPEN THE
DOOR TO NEW
EXPERIENCES.

SOMETIMES IT'S THROUGH
THE WORDS OF OTHERS
THAT WE FIND OURSELVES.

SONG LYRIC THERAPY — USING LYRICS TO COPE WITH YOUR EMOTIONS — IS A POWERFUL TOOL FOR SELF-HEALING. PAY ATTENTION TO THE LYRICS OF YOUR FAVORITE SONGS (OR SEEK OUT SOME NEW ONES!) AND NOTICE HOW THEY SPEAK TO YOU. WORDS ARE MIGHTY LITTLE THINGS, AND THE WORDS OTHERS HAVE WRITTEN CAN HELP YOU CONNECT WITH WHAT YOU'RE FEELING, IN BOTH GOOD TIMES AND BAD.

TRY NOT TO
LET MEMORIES
OF WHAT WAS
TAKE YOU AWAY
FROM WHAT IS.

today

april

YOU CAN BEGIN AGAIN AT ANY TIME! HERE'S WHAT YOU'LL NEED:

- A BIT OF INSPIRATION (TO KEEP YOU MOVING FORWARD)

- A TOUCH OF COURAGE (AFTER ALL, STARTING AGAIN IS BRAVE!)

- A DASH OF HUSTLE (SO THAT YOU CAN STAY MOTIVATED)

- SPRINKLING OF CREATIVITY (LETTING GO OF THE OLD MEANS CRAFTING THE NEW)

- A HEAP OF FOCUS (JUST SO YOU KEEP YOUR EYE ON THE PRIZE!)

GIVE OUT MORE OF WHAT
YOU WANT TO GET BACK.

WITH EVERY NEW CALENDAR COMES AN OPPORTUNITY TO PONDER THE PAST AND PLAN FOR THE FUTURE. WHILE THE PRESENT IS THE VERY BEST PLACE TO SPEND YOUR TIME, IT NEVER HURTS TO ALLOW YOURSELF TIME FOR REFLECTION. YOU HAVE COME A LONG WAY SINCE LAST YEAR – AND YOU'LL GO EVEN FURTHER IN THE YEAR TO COME. YOU HAVE HAD HIGHS AND YOU HAVE HAD LOWS, AND STILL, YOU ARE HERE. THAT, IN ITSELF, IS A REMARKABLE THING.

WINTER WISHLIST

WISDOM: SEEK OUT THE INSIGHTS FOUND IN THE WORLD ALL AROUND YOU.

INSPIRATION: PINPOINT (AND TRY TO SPEND TIME SURROUNDED BY) WHAT MOVES YOU.

STRENGTH: LOOK FOR THE MOTIVATION TO KEEP PUSHING FORWARD.

FINAL THOUGHTS...

ACCEPTANCE. BALANCE. CHANGE. THESE ARE THE THREE LESSONS THAT ECHO THROUGHOUT EACH SEASON. EVERY SEASON IS AN OPPORTUNITY TO ACCEPT WHAT IS, TO SEEK BALANCE, AND TO EMBRACE CHANGE. DOING SO IS THE VERY BEST METHOD I'VE FOUND FOR GROWING THROUGH THE SEASONS OF LIFE. GROWTH (EVEN THE GOOD KIND) CAN BE UNCOMFORTABLE, AND I HOPE THIS BOOK HAS PROVIDED YOU WITH INSPIRATION AS YOU GO THROUGH LIFE'S UPS AND DOWNS.

EVEN AS YOU TUCK THIS BOOK AWAY ON YOUR SHELF, I HOPE YOU REMEMBER THAT GROWTH TAKES TIME AND THAT WONDERFUL THINGS CAN HAPPEN WHEN YOU LEAST EXPECT THEM TO. I HOPE YOU REMEMBER THAT THERE ARE SEASONS OF THRIVING AND SEASONS OF REST. I HOPE YOU ACCEPT THAT THERE WILL BE TIMES WHEN YOU ARE FLOURISHING AND TIMES WHEN YOU FEEL WITHERED. I HOPE YOU KEEP IN MIND THAT NO SEASON WILL LAST FOREVER.

I HOPE YOU ENJOY YOUR BEST MOMENTS AND TRY TO LEARN FROM YOUR WORST. (I HOPE, TOO, THAT YOU'RE KIND TO YOURSELF EVEN WHEN YOU DON'T DO THIS.) I HOPE YOU ALLOW YOURSELF TO BE RIGHT WHERE YOU ARE, EVEN WHEN IT'S NOT NECESSARILY WHERE YOU WANT TO BE. AND, MOST OF ALL, I HOPE THAT, NO MATTER WHAT SEASON YOU FIND YOURSELF IN, YOU FIND A WAY TO GROW THROUGH IT.

ABOUT THE AUTHOR

DANI DIPIRRO IS AN AUTHOR AND ILLUSTRATOR LIVING IN A SUBURB OF WASHINGTON, DC.

IN 2009, SHE LAUNCHED THE WEBSITE POSITIVELYPRESENT.COM TO SHARE HER INSIGHTS ABOUT LIVING A POSITIVE AND PRESENT LIFE.

DANI IS ALSO THE AUTHOR OF <u>EVERYDAY OPTIMISM: HOW TO BE PRESENT AND POSITIVE AT WORK, AT HOME, AND IN LOVE</u>; <u>STAY POSITIVE: DAILY REMINDERS FROM POSITIVELY PRESENT</u>; AND THE EFFORTLESS INSPIRATION SERIES.

DANI ALSO SHARES HER TALENTS AS AN ILLUSTRATOR ON HER POPULAR INSTAGRAM ACCOUNT. FOLLOW HER AT @POSITIVELYPRESENT. TO LEARN MORE ABOUT DANI, VISIT POSITIVELYPRESENT.COM.